The Little Girl Pepper

CATHERINE WALKER

WESTBOW
PRESS®
A DIVISION OF THOMAS NELSON
& ZONDERVAN

WestBow Press books may be ordered through
booksellers or by contacting:

WestBow Press
A Division of Thomas Nelson & Zondervan
1663 Liberty Drive
Bloomington, IN 47403
www.westbowpress.com
844-714-3454

Scripture quotations marked NKJV are taken from the
New King James Version®. Copyright © 1982 by Thomas
Nelson. Used by permission. All rights reserved.

ISBN: 978-1-9736-6542-7 (sc)
ISBN: 978-1-9736-6541-0 (e)

Print information available on the last page.

WestBow Press rev. date: 09/15/2020

Part I

The Little Girl Pepper

SO, OUR LITTLE GIRL PEPPER IS FIVE YEARS old. My husband and I and Pepper had just settled in for the evening from work and school. While we were in the kitchen, the little curious one went to the recreation room. I heard typing on the computer. It was Pepper, typing very fast. It was unbelievable.

It took my husband and me by surprise. I went into the room and asked Pepper, "What are you doing?" "Mother, I am researching some things," Pepper replied. "Ok," I said. While I was on my way to work, and getting ready to drop Pepper off at daycare, Pepper asked me a question. "Mother, can I be anything I want to be when I grow-up?"

"Yes," I replied. "Baby, you can be whatever you want. What do you want to be? My little woman is very smart." Pepper answered, "I want to be a doctor like you, and a lawyer like father." "Really!" I said, astonished. Pepper continued, "I want to help people in every way I can, so, if I am both, I can heal them and protect them at the same time." Pepper's mother was amazed by the wisdom of such a young child. The reaction from her little mouth was so amazing that her mother looked at her with disbelief, wondering if she was her little Pepper. Already sounding grown. It's like she had been here before. Who are you? I thought. I couldn't help but chuckle. "Pepper, when I pick you up this evening, you and I and your father will sit and talk about what you want to be, ok," I said. "Yes, Mother, I would like that. I can't wait, because time is going so fast. I will be a grown-up before you know it," she responded. I thought, Oh my goodness what have we got on our hands? A genius! I called my husband and told him exactly what Pepper said and he told me that he will be there so that we both can speak with her. My husband jokingly said, "Honey, she's only five years old going on twenty."

After work, I picked up Pepper at the daycare, and she was in rare form. I asked, "What's up with you, baby girl? "Did you have a great day?" "Yes, Mother, I did," she answered. Pepper continued, "Are we going to talk about my career when we get home?" "Yes, we are," I said. "Daddy will be there too. When we got home, Hugh, my husband, was there already." He greeted us, "Hi, pumpkin." Pepper replied, "Daddy, why do you call me that?" "Because you are my little pumpkin," Hugh responded. Her father continued, "Pumpkin, we want to talk with you because I understand you want to be a lawyer and a doctor." Pepper said, "Yes, that's what I want to be. Did mother tell you why?" "Yes, she did, and I thought it was a great idea if that's what you want," her father said. "Father, I know how I can do this. Listen, let me tell you," she said. "Yes, baby, tell Mom and Dad," her father said eagerly. Pepper explained, "I researched all avenues and this is how I am going about it. I will be both a lawyer and a doctor by studying a normal four-year BA or BS, and then I will go to medical school and study medicine for five years of internship, and from seven years to eight years of residency. Then I will go to law school for another three years. Then I will take the state exams on the knowledge of medicine and the exams for the knowledge of the law. It will not be easy, but a few people have done it before. Both are professional degrees. I know me. I will and I can, because this is what I want to be when I grow up." Her father wanted an IQ test for her like yesterday.

Afterwards, Pepper's mom and dad were standing in the kitchen talking about how they can support their daughter in realizing her dreams. Pepper got a hold one of her mom's medical books on the vascular system and was leafing through the pages. After reading the book, she ran excitedly into the kitchen. "Mother," she said, "How does gravity affect the body's vascular system?" Hugh was stunned by Pepper's question. Her question showed a level of deep thinking not typical of a 5-year old. The next day they went in for an IQ test. Pepper's IQ was 160. Pepper's mother had a good feeling that's what it would be. She was both excited and sad about the high IQ. She had noticed that everything came naturally for Pepper. On the other hand, she was losing all the moments of her daughter's childhood. Pepper asked her mother, "Why did I need to take that test?" Her mom replied, "Pepper, you are a very intelligent little girl, and your dad and I wanted to know so we can do our part as your mom and dad. Her dad thought to himself, It scares me to the point, I fear for her well-being. So, what's in the future for this intelligent little girl? This 5-year old blows me away with her body and big brain fully powerful with all that knowledge." Pepper said to her mom and dad, "I am good. I am not in any pain, so you don't need to take me to another doctor." Her mom reassured her by saying, "No baby, we are not going to take you to any more doctors, ok." Pepper asked, "Mom, can I go to the recreation room and get on the computer for a while?" "Of course," here mom answered. Pepper's mother thought, it's almost like having a child that has difficulty learning. Maybe, I am just confused. Hugh was also deep in his own thoughts. He didn't know about his daughter's goals and dreams until his wife told him. It was like it happened overnight. Hugh called his mom and dad and decided to visit with them in a few days. After talking to his parents, Hugh told his wife, "My mom has some videos to show us and maybe that would make us feel a lot better."

They visited Hugh's mom and dad and had dinner with them. It was delicious. Afterwards, they watched the videos. Hugh said in a surprised tone, "They are about me!" He was also an intelligent child, so smart that his mother had the same problem they were now having with Pepper. Hugh thought, I could not believe that I was that child. Hugh's Mom said, "Just let that baby be herself and do what makes her happy. She will be just fine." Turning her attention to her granddaughter, Hugh's mother said, "Pepper, come see grandma." Pepper said, "Okay, grandma, I'm coming." Pepper sat down beside her grandma. Her grandma asked, "What were you researching on your computer? Pepper said, "Some things." Grandma said, "Oh, but your parents told me you want to be a doctor and a lawyer." Then, Pepper began to reveal her dreams to her grandpa and grandma. After listening to Pepper tell about her future plans, Grandma said to Pepper's parents, "I see now son, why you and Raven are so worried about this baby. Maybe you need to ask her first-grade teacher about what she thinks about Pepper."

A few days later, Pepper's parents went to the daycare and spoke with Pepper's teacher, Mrs. West. The teacher explained that Pepper is very intelligent, and that Pepper tutors the other children in the class. Mrs. West said, "I let her teach the other students; otherwise, I believe that Pepper would be bored, and I want all the students to be engaged and learning." As the meeting wrapped up, Mrs. West said, "Mr. and Mrs. Brown, we will administer a reading test to Pepper to determine her grade level. Another thing you may want to think about is putting her in a gifted school. They have them on the Westside of town. Please keep me informed. I would like to keep up with Pepper's progress because I care about her very much." Mrs. Brown said, "We will let you know everything." Pepper's parent told Mrs. West that Pepper was already given an IQ test and her score is 160. Now, based on her IQ score, her age, and the result of the reading test, all the stakeholders agreed to schedule a follow-up meeting to determine Pepper's grade level placement.

After the results of the reading test came back, it was determined that Pepper was reading at a high school level. Her parents, Mrs. West, and her guidance counselor all decided that Pepper would be placed in the 10th grade with constant assistant.

Mr. Brown called his mother, "Hello, mother, I called to let you know about your granddaughter. We took her for an IQ test, and she scored 160. I was astonished by the outcome." His mother was not too surprised because of her experience with him. She simply said, "I thought as much, son." He continued, "Mother, I think we need to seek counseling for our family. "What do you think of that?" His mom replied, "That's a good idea." Hugh said to his mother, "This little genius is about to blow the doors off the hinge. But mother she's only five years old." Mrs. Brown chimed in and added, "Pepper's first grade teacher told Hugh and me during our conference that she often stepped back, while Pepper navigates new challenges to broaden her understanding. Her teacher said Pepper took it upon herself to teach the other students in the class. His mother exclaimed, "What!" "You and Hugh will need to spend more time with Pepper because she still needs to be cuddled and comforted by her mother and father. We know she will have a great deal of time away from the familiarity of home due to the high school schedule. You know, at her young age, she will increasingly express a desire to be independent, however, communication will be the key to Pepper's well-being. Because of my experience with you, Hugh, I believe that these are some of the things that will facilitate the milestones of Pepper's growth and development." Hugh felt encouraged by his mother's wisdom and felt that Pepper would be just fine.

On her first day in the tenth grade at Academy School for the Gifted Pepper arrived with her personal teacher assistant, who will be with her throughout her time in high school. Hugh reminded his wife to contact Raven's daycare teacher. "Raven, would you stop by and tell Mrs. West about Pepper?" Raven replied, "I called her this morning and she was very happy."

Pepper completed high school at age 9. She went on to the college as a preteen. She received a full scholarship. She went on and got her degrees and became a lawyer and doctor. Mrs. Brown said, "When Pepper came home, she was all grown-up and just as beautiful and intelligent as we thought she would be. We are so proud of her." Pepper's parents bought her the building for her Law Practice so that she could put the right people in place. She's regarded as one the best, World-class neurosurgery in the northern Virginia area. Her parents are happy for her that she's doing what she loves. At this point, she is only 20 years old.

Mrs. Brown stopped by to see Pepper at her law office. They greeted each other warmly. Pepper said, "Mother, remember when I asked you about the vascular system?" Her mother replied, "Yes baby, I do remember." "That was important for me to ask you. It stuck in my head. Now I am the best doctor in my specialty, a fellowship-trained expert in diseases and conditions affecting the spine. Pepper said. "Well, I know all about that now. I knew that was my calling." Mother and daughter said goodbye to each other.

First, I travel through the early years of life's lesson that were timeless. I decided to take a walk and ended up on top of the hill of this beautiful mountain. So I kept on going to see where I would end up. It was quite an adventure to see the beautiful artwork that was before me. So as I heard in my head the sounds of music floating somewhere on a long road to relief. It's just like a picture book. This came to mind to be thankful for every mountain because it's the mountaintop that will give me the best view of the world. It's beautiful. I looked over to my right and saw amazing things that I could not refuse. I don't know what was ahead, but I kept ongoing. Oh wow! I looked over to my right and then the left. Over there, what is that? I ask myself. The further I went up on the mountain the better it looked. There are some other people over there. Look! Look! I wanted to go over and introduce myself. It was about twenty people in a group, so I began talking and getting some great information. I also saw a lot of businesses. This one place stopped me in my track. It was the most beautiful Medical center of all time. I would like to work there someday. As I appeared to get what I needed to work in that amazing centerpiece of the world. I looked over and saw the big beautiful building, the Spinal Surgical Fellowship Program. At this center they provide the most comprehensive training in the world. This is great. What a journey! I went there and spoke with several doctors. Oh, my goodness, the things that I learned! The doctors there gave me a tour of surgeries that were being done, including for deformity of the disc, and other degenerative conditions affecting the spine, tumors, trauma, and arthritis with such treatments as endoscopic, microscopic, and minimally invasive surgeries. The fellowship consists of both inpatient and outpatient. I realize that his is where I want to be. I am going to be the best. I have the knowledge to do all that. The specialists collaborate with the entire healthcare team, including neurologists, orthopedists, radiologists, and pain control specialists, oncologists, and primary care physicians. I feel right at home knowing that I can help many more patients by working with these amazing physicians.

One day, Pepper called her mother after work. Her mother was concerned that she was spending more time at her doctor's office, so she asked her, "How are you doing with your law clients?" Pepper replied, "I got them all lined up as well." Her mother asked, "What time will you be home, baby?" "I will have your dinner, ready, ok mother." "Thank you. See you soon." Dinner was served and Pepper and her parents talked about what was going on with her. Her father wanted to know when is there going to be a young man in her life? Pepper told him that she had met someone, and that he is a Cardiologist and a Neurologist. "Oh!" Her father replied. "When are we going to meet this young man?" "Soon," Pepper replied. "Right now, we are very busy because of his double specialty." After dinner, Pepper called Brad, the young man she was dating. She told him that her parents wanted to meet him and he agreed to meet them that weekend.

Pepper told her mother that she spoke with Brad and he said the weekend would work with his schedule. "How about Saturday evening," Pepper asked. Her mother replied, "Yes, that's great." Her mother asked, "What does he like to eat, Pepper?" She answered, "He likes fresh salmon, chicken, fresh vegetables, and green salad with ranch dressing." Her mother said, "That's almost identical to what you father wants. On Saturday, they all sat down to dinner and had a long talk. Pepper said, "We are going to open the west wing of the hospital. We had a meeting today and they said this wing will hold several thousand people. We need that west wing. So, many sick people. Also, I was thinking about going back to school." Astonished, Pepper's mom, said, "Oh my goodness, Pepper!" "Don't you think you are taking on too much? Talk to her Brad." Brad replied, "You know, Mother Raven she has her mind already made up. She loves her work." Pepper said excitedly, "Oh, father, I just got fifteen clients today, I will be very busy for the month and I have four court cases next week, so what going on with you Brad." Brad answered, "Well, I have quite a few surgeries next week." Pepper added, "The west wing is going to be for Brad's patients." Her mother exclaimed, "What?" Pepper responded, "Yes, thanks to Brad's parents, he's the owner of the west wing." "Congratulations, Brad!" Mr. and Mrs. Brown said at the same time. "Thank you," Brad said. "My parents donated the west wing to the hospital as my graduation present. Neurologists need to work closely with patients to diagnose and treat clinical disorders of the human nervous system. I take my job seriously and love to give my patients the best care possible, this includes brain injuries. Most of all my patients need friendly communication because some feel uncomfortable. Like Pepper, I want to go back to school. I'm going back this fall to continue research in the field of neurology to find new medical advancements that could potentially work as treatments." Pepper said, "Mom and I were talking about gaining higher education and becoming an expert in my chosen fields, but she pointed out that being skillful, while beneficial to my patients can be detrimental to my own health and wellbeing." Mr. Brown said, "My little pumpkin battles to be the brightest and the best at whatever she does. Pepper, we just want to let you know that we love you and support you in everything you want out of life." "Thanks, Dad," Pepper said. After dinner, Pepper and Brad got ready to leave her parents' home. Brad said, "Pepper, would you like to go out with some friends?" Pepper replied, "Yes." "Where are you guys going?" Brad replied, "We were thinking about that club on West Moorland Street." "Oh yes," Pepper said. "Sandra told me she had been there, and the atmosphere is great." Brad said, so it will be Sandra, Mike, Jerry, Wanda, Timothy,

Gail, Lucy, Allen, and us. I am going to call and make a reservation for 10 people." They went to the club and had a good time catching up with some friends they rarely see because of everyone's demanding careers. As time went on, they were dating all the time. Finally, Pepper told her mom and dad that she was serious about Brad. They dated for two years and Brad asked Pepper to marry him, and she said yes. Her parents were glad because they felt she was working too hard. Pepper and her mom planned the wedding and it was a big one. Pepper had ten bridesmaids and ten groomsmen. Her colors were serenity, a soft blue, and white. It was a beautiful wedding. Five hundred guests were invited. Pepper and Brad went to Paris for their honeymoon. They visited the usual tourist sites and enjoyed delicious French cuisine. When Pepper and Brad came home from Paris, they moved into a five-bedroom house, which was a wedding gift from Brad's parents.

In a conversation with her mother after she returned from her honeymoon, Pepper's mother said, "That house is an amazing and beautiful blessing. Pepper, I am so happy for you both." Pepper said, "Now, we can go forward with our love of the medical field, and my commitment to my law practice. Brad is doing quite well, as well. We thank God for the responsible employees we have working for our businesses. We knew what we wanted out of life at a very young age, so it wasn't about the what, it was how. To move forward in life, we needed a firm foundation. Understanding what and where we wanted to go in life will provide us a vision and a spirit to keep it moving forward. By the end of the year, we are going to open a ward in our hospital for people without healthcare coverage. I will need to hire more specialists. We have a program headed up by my husband, Brad, on getting some interns right out of college."

Finally, the new wing at the hospital was completed and Pepper and Brad hired ten different kinds of specialists from all over the world. Being a conservative in her field of medical care isn't inherently bad. But for many of her patients, this could mean forgoing necessary care and putting themselves at risk because of the lack of medical coverage. The new wing is going to be called the Pepper Brown Medical Health Services. Pepper and Brad can afford to financially take care of the patients who are uncovered, so they decided to do just that because they are able to do it, and they love doing it. Many patients have said that Pepper and Brad are the most giving people in the world. After several years of success with their businesses, Brad and Pepper decided to start a family.

Pepper and Brad had twin boys and later had twin girls and they were all very intelligent children like their parents. "Here it goes again." though Pepper. Pepper said to Brad, "Now, we know what our parents went through when we were born." They decided to have both set of twins tested before they started school. Both set of twins were placed in the 3rd grade when they were four years old at the Gifted School on the Westside of town their attended. Isn't it funny where our journey leads us? One part of our journey is unfolding whether or not we are aware of it. The other part requires our active participation in our growth. The first part is what occurs naturally as we go through life. We make choices, and through these life-choices, we become established. Pepper has found, that throughout her life, she found that there can be much spiritual development if we choose to take an active part in our spiritual well-being. She believes that this is what we are instructed to do. Brad often said that taking steps with God is a solid reason why God blesses us financially, showing his Love, confirming his covenant for his Kingdom in order for people to be blessed. Also, this differentiates God's children from others, and ultimately for His Glory. Therefore, when God blesses us financially, we should not raise our standard of living, we should raise our standard of giving. In 2 Corinthians 9:8 (NKJV), it states, "And God is able to make all grace abound toward you, that you, always having all sufficiency in all things, may have an abundance for every good work."

Part 2

The Little Girl Pepper

———◦⚬✸⚬◦———

PEPPER HAS BEEN ON A PHENOMENAL journey over the years striving to be a Christian woman and touching the hearts of many others like herself. She understands that we have all had our tender moments because of our struggles in life. Pepper has had lots of milestones on her journey, yet she continues to further her success story. She had once told her parents that the longest journey she wanted to make in life is from her head to her heart. Her father had told her that it is especially true in transferring the knowledge about God in your head to being able to experience the excitement of a loving God in your heart. Her mother had mentioned that she, too, is on the same journey trying to understand the tremendous odds against us in transferring the truth about God's love and possessing it as a feeling of love in our soul. Her mother had encouraged her to use her genius mind to do as the Bible said to, "go and teach others". With that being said, if you know about the love of God in your head, you should also feel and experience the presence and love of God in your heart. Pepper's parents told her many times that they were proud of her and what she is trying to do, and she told them that she was thankful to them for their guidance and love. Pepper recognized the talents and gifts that her Heavenly Father had graciously poured into her as well as blessing her with nurturing supporting parents. She expressed her gratitude daily by using her gifts to benefit others and glorifying God.

Second Touch

"**Y**OU SEE, MY CHRISTIAN WALK IS LIKE the wind," Pepper said. John 3:8, NKJV, "The wind blows wherever it pleases. You hear its sound, but you cannot tell where it's coming from or where it is going. So it is with everyone born of the spirit." Speaking of her faith, Pepper said, "First of all, my Christian walk is to completely surrender my entire life to God, the Father. Jesus should become Lord over your life, as well your Savior. The Christian walk is like the wind being in control of your life. It means having realistic expectations and accepting the challenges while on your journey. The most important ingredient to living a healthy and happy rewarding life is to love one another. Love is like the wind. You can't see it, but you always feel it! You see, the problem isn't finding out where you are going, but figuring out what you are going to do after you get there. Then again maybe God has a bigger and better plan for us than we have for ourselves. It's like the Evolving Endeavor has moved! When rising in the morning, I get on my knees and pray this prayer to my Heavenly Father, 'I stretch my hands to thee, no other help I know; If Thou withdraw thyself from me, Ah! Whither shall I go?' I remembered a time, being so different I had a special way about myself, and my friends would always say you are very strange. I love them no matter what. Most of my friends have stayed the same and when I started growing and evolving, our relationships changed. My spiritual growth challenged their lifestyle because I am no longer doing worldly things with them. When I became active in my outreach, they started questioning everything. Unfortunately, when it came to questioning their own lives, things became so uncomfortable that they changed the topic and turned the conversation back to me and how weird I seem to them now. But they also think I am fun, amazing, beautiful, lovely, and of course inspirational. I know it is truly God! He has a strong presence in my heart. You see, to trust God means that he has total control of our lives. When someone comes along and interrupts your state of mind that causes pain. Most of the time it's a friend from church, or a family member whose values differ from yours, but uses you to get what they want. I love those people from a distance. Then you ask yourself how many friendships have been shattered because their cruel words or actions left you with a feeling of betrayal? I love with my whole heart and soul. In some areas of the Christian life, we struggle to find out how God wants us to respond. I've searched all over and I came to the conclusion that I am an intellectual and serious person. For the people who are trying to stop my blessings, let me take you on a journey. There is a scenic spot that I often travel to. It's a long bank of that pathway where I make my deposits. You see scripture gives us words of encouragement and hope as we go through this journey. I understand the teaching of the Lord and how he puts his words into my heart. In Romans 12:14 NJKV it states, "Bless those who persecute you; bless and do not curse." Also the Bible says in Romans 12:20-21, "Therefore if your enemy is hungry, feed him; if he is thirsty, give him a drink: For in so doing you will heap coals of fire on his head. Do not be overcome by evil but overcome evil with good." It's very counterintuitive and it's very difficult to do, but it works. I've learned that God's instructions are detailed, and most Christian intellectuals have seriously deluded themselves about their importance and capabilities. I hate to admit that there is somethings we can't do or understand. And we must understand that it isn't about us reaching God, it's about God reaching us. Jesus is the way to Salvation with fear and trembling. Salvation is just the beginning. God has a perfect plan and destiny for my life. Once you become saved and born again, God will set you on an incredible adventure. I know that's what Revelation is all about. People can seek all they want, but unless God chooses to reveal himself, we have no hope of ever knowing God. Thank you, Jesus I know my savior lives in me because I can feel him in my soul."

Pepper continued to think about her spiritual

growth and said, "Sometimes I get overwhelmed because of my love of music. When I joined the choir, the first thing I needed to learn was the rules of the Music Ministry. I stepped out on faith without the knowledge of music. That's exactly how it works with God, you don't need to know the rules of any playing field because God is omnipotent. I will keep my mind, body, and soul in the Word of God."

Knowledge is Power

THINKING ABOUT HER LIVED EXPERIENCE, Pepper said, "At a young age, my education prepared me for life-long learning. As a child, I wanted to grow up to be a smart young woman. If I saw a book, I would pick it up and start reading, or if I was working on a math problem, I would keep trying until I figured it out. I relied on God and had faith in myself to prepare for my life's work. Even as a child, I was passionate about the position and direction of my life. I persevered, and when moments of decision were upon me, I never felt stressed out or confused. While I was preparing and planning for my career, I tried to breathe, relax, and enjoy the journey. Throughout the process, I relied on God's preparation so that I could perform and not be anxious or filled with doubt. A person's mind is the greatest gift God has given to us, and it ought to be devoted entirely to Him. We should seek to ". . .[bring] every thought into captivity to the obedience of Christ" (2 Corinthians 10:5). This will be one of the greatest assets of a person's faith when a time of trial comes because then a person's faith and the Spirit of God will work together for God's glory. At church one Sunday, the preacher was setting the atmosphere for the Holy Spirit to come in and he read Hebrews 12:6-10. I was ready to hear the Word. The pastor gave us the title of his sermon: "God's Unconditional Love." The pastor said, "When you look in the mirror, what do you see?" I imagined that I saw the keys to my goals, and I played them up. I realized that I had the power to accomplish my goals, and I thank God for His blessings. The preacher continued, "You see, most of us hate the things that make us different from everyone else rather than embrace them. Christians can be influenced by an evil spirit. There are all sorts of spiritual activity going on in the atmosphere and at times if you are not walking in the spirit and sensitive to the spirit and discerning of spirits, you can be influenced and all of a sudden come up with a thought that is alien to you in the natural. It is like the thought just shot into your mind and you wonder where it came from. Sometimes people around you who are bound by strong demons that can affect you. The soul of a man can pick up on these spirits like a radio pick up radio waves from the air that we can't see. The spirit working in and through others, at times, affect others around them, without possessing them, almost like the radio waves. There is something the soul of a man can pick up or be influenced by. You can go into a certain place, whether a church or a bar, a hotel or a house, and sense a certain atmosphere that has to do with what the people are thinking and what is going on within them. Are they full of strife, contention, or hatred? It can be picked up and you can be influenced by it in the spirit. Some children when they come close to people with demons will, all of a sudden, start acting differently or change their behavior. Their soul is picking up and is being influenced by the spiritual activity around them. Be aware that demons cannot do their work without a person. Demons work through people because it gives them a voice to speak through." The pastor concluded his sermon and prayed for the congregation.

The next day, after that sermon, Pepper said, "I crawled out of bed. It was a sunny day. The clouds were crystal clear, and the trees were bright green. It had rained the night before. I could see that the leaves were perfectly shaped. I calmly spoke to God. I said, "Lord God, I need you to come quickly." I waited and He showed up after I had gone to the prayer closet, a small room off from my bedroom." A prayer closet is designed to be a private room for prayer. "I was stunned I felt like the spirit of God showed up very quickly. Oh, my God!" I said. I thought it was a dream or I was walking in my sleep. It wasn't a dream or a fuzzy experience in any way. He was there, as plainly as day and night. Did I see Him with my eyes? No. Hear Him with ears? No. But I felt Him and heard Him loud and clear, nonetheless. I call this a revelation, and it's like nothing else. In my mind, this experience went on for days. It was unbelievable but didn't seem unnatural in the least. It didn't occur to me until afterward that this should have seemed strange to me. I did not know what to say. I was very quiet for a while just thinking about what I had experienced with Jesus talking to me and what the pastor had said in his sermon. Eventually, it became clear to me that the Creator loves us all and that He is dependable."

Because of God Grace

EPPER CONTINUED THINKING ABOUT
her spiritual journey saying, "As I enter into
God's grace, I think of how blessed I am to have
a Heavenly Father. Everything I have is because
of Him, a gracious gift from God. That's why
I feel "overjoyed" and abundantly free, to say I
serve a mighty God. I am at ease in giving Him
my all and all without any hesitation. I know
and have learned that Jesus gave up his riches in
heaven so that through His poverty, we might
become rich. Now, I realize what the book of
Hebrews, Chapter 4: 1-13 NKJV said. It is a book
that tests my courage in a sense. I can honestly
say that I appreciate the gift of faithfulness, and

the power of God's greatness in my life now and forevermore. So why not feel blessed in having great insight into many things? I believe that waiting is one of God's most powerful tools of grace. God doesn't just give us grace for waiting. He gave us the gift of grace to strengthen us while we are waiting. So waiting is not only about what you will receive at the end of it.

You see, I pondered my journey in this life and it gives me a sense of direction. I try not to lose sight of the landmarks that guide me on my travels. I used to get sad when I would think about life because that I was a little afraid of what was ahead if me. I knew that I would start to enjoy the journey the closer I got to my destination. When the rain or cloudy days would come upon me, it would obscure my vision, but I would think of God's Words of encouragement, and His loving protection for me that protected me from the storms that assailed me. A healthy mind causes us to breathe easily and when you own your circumstances, you are in control. And I can say to myself, congratulation I have won the victory! Thank you, God for your light as I travel through this tunnel of life. I am grateful for your small voice that leads me to the place where I am in your presence so that I can walk this narrow road another day. I am confident that my walk with God is not a lonely walk. Luke 1:79 says, "To give light to those who sit in darkness and the shadow of death, to guide our feet into the way of peace."

Assurance of Blessings

PEPPER'S REFLECTION CONTINUES, "THE scriptures teach me that we can know with certainty that we have the life of God within us. In the Word, this confidence is not based on inner feelings or outward signs. Rather, this "Blessed Assurance" is founded upon the promises of a faithful God and His inspired Word. It depends not on the amount of our faith but the object of our faith, Christ himself. Sometimes we are not careful of despairing about ourselves because we forget that we are commanded to put our trust in God and not ourselves. And still today our hearts are inspired to seek God and our spirits lifted as we sing or make our testimonies

41

together for the benefit of our lives. You see, we are striving to uphold the honor of His name by diligence to realize the full assurance of hope. If we don't stay in the word, we can lose out on the most important aspect of the Christian life, which is the power of God. I feel a sense of urgency in directing my focus to serving God by being patient and showing endurance. In doing so, I will maintain the full assurance of hope and love of the Lord. The way I receive my gift of God's empowerment is by my actions and efforts. And because of His promises, I know my God is everything I want in this world."

Responsibility

P EPPER CONCLUDES HER CONTEMPLATION, "Life can be a lot easier than we think. We have a responsibility to God to be faithful, therefore, we do not need to accept anyone else's opinion about anything. We all have a conscience. Our conscience is the voice of God within us, and we must listen to it and obey it. We should be willing to help others, not only because it feels good, but God commands us to help one another. As a neurosurgeon, I respect my patients' as well as their families' health and wellbeing. Therefore, I consider it a sacred responsibility to use my ability, the expertise of my assistants, and the latest technology to offer the best medical care possible while keeping in mind their individual values and preferences. Having a two-way communication with my patients is vitally important because as much as I need to talk to my patients, it's equally important for them to talk to me. Christ spent his time on earth preaching that we are to take care of those who are less fortunate. Also, I know instinctively that the one God I serve is loving and forgiving. Christianity teaches me to love everyone. It is not exclusionary or elite. It is as the Bible says, "God is love." 1 John 4:8 NKJV. The sooner we realize that, accept that, and integrate that into our work ethic, then we will be on our way to being successful. Romans 8:31 (NKJV) "What then shall we say to these things? If God is for us, who can be against us?"

Acknowledgements

IAM THANKFUL TO THE ALMIGHTY GOD who orchestrated the course of my life. For the blessings of my family and my friends I am eternally grateful. Writing became a passion for me when my walking buddy encouraged me to write down my thoughts daily. It was the release I needed. I am grateful to Paulette Garner for being that inspiration, for reading this book, and helping me to edit it.

Printed in the United States
By Bookmasters